MW01232635

A LIFE LIVED

THE STORY OF WILLIAM "BILL" BLAIR FROM THE NEGRO BASEBALL LEAGUE TO NEWSPAPER PUBLISHER.

WILLIAM "BILL" BLAIR

authorHOUSE®

AuthorHouse™
1663 Liberty Drive
Bloomington, IN 47403
www.authorhouse.com
Phone: 1-800-839-8640

Published by AuthorHouse 12/19/2013

ISBN: 978-1-4918-3410-7 (sc)
ISBN: 978-1-4918-3409-1 (e)

INTRODUCTION

A S YOU WILL READ IN THIS autobiography, William Blair is a Dallas icon and legend. In a city where the names of white politicians and businessmen dominate its landscape, its buildings, and its institutions, only a handful of African-American names have earned the same status. While the city's freeways and institutions bear names such as John Stemmons, Erik Jonsson, Robert L. Thornton, and Marvin D. Love, the sites that recognize its African-American icons and legends, such as A. Maceo, Smith, George Allen, J.C. Phelps, and Juanita Craft, are few. In 2011, William Blair joined this list of icons and legends when the city named a park for him in South Dallas.

With this new autobiography we learn why he has become such an icon and legend. His story is unique. As someone who has spent all but seven of his 90+ years in Dallas he has made his mark on the city. He attended Booker T. Washington High School when it was the only high school in the city open to African Americans. As an athlete, he starred in football and baseball. After a short, but successful career as a pitcher with the Indianapolis Clowns in the Negro Baseball League he returned to Dallas and started two newspapers. The second newspaper, *The Elite News*, became his *magnum opus* and he has published it for over fifty years. Like many African-American businessmen who preceded him, he found a niche market and served it when others ridiculed and criticized his efforts for doing so.

The story of William Blair's life is both an African-American autobiographical narrative and a story about black Dallas. Reading it one learns about the hardships of growing up in a segregated society. From his experiences growing up in Dallas's State-Thomas neighborhood, interacting with other African Americans and whites to his six-year sojourn with the Indianapolis Clowns to his emergence as one of the Dallas's most influential newspaper publishers, we learn how an African American had to navigate and negotiate a society that treated him as a second class citizen. We learn about his family life and the parenting and educational standards that shaped his life. Blair illustrates how the parenting that he received and the educational instruction and coaching that he received from his teachers and coaches in Dallas's segregated, educational system taught him valuable lessons, shaped his life, and influenced his path toward adulthood.

On the one hand, Blair's story is one that is similar to that of many African Americans who came of age in Dallas in the early twentieth century. But, on the other hand, it is also a very unique story because of his perseverance and success in overcoming the obstacles that he confronted as an African American in Dallas. Perhaps the most revealing and insightful part of his story is his description of his relationship with one of the city's powerbrokers—Reverend S. M. Wright, pastor of People's Missionary Baptist Church and leader of the influential Interdenominational Ministerial Alliance (IMA). Reverend Wright's critical contemporaries and lay biographers have reviled him as an "accommodationist" like Booker T. Washington and as one of the city African-American leaders who refused to challenge Dallas's "white power structure." But Blair presents Reverend Wright as a much more nuanced and complex figure in Dallas's racial politics. Indeed, as Blair presents him, Reverend Wright is not so much an "accommodationist" as an African-American leader attempting to balance the needs of his community and his congregation with the realities of the city's conservative politics dominated by white businessmen. Blair's personal assessment of Reverend Wright, one of Dallas's most important African-American powerbrokers, makes his story a must read for historians writing about Dallas in the twentieth century and its adjustment to desegregation.

Finally, I must add a personal note about William Blair. I met William Blair in 1985 at Graham's Barbershop in South Dallas where he "held court" on a regular basis to discuss the Dallas political scene. On one occasion he was criticizing one of my favorite Dallas African-American politicians and expressing an opposition to him and his politics that astounded me. Later, I found that Blair and the local politician were engaged in an ongoing, personal conflict including a lawsuit. I spoke up in defense of the local politician and Blair put me in my place in no uncertain terms. Of course, I learned then that "Mr. Blair was being Mr. Blair," and that he did not take anything from anyone, including a junior college professor. As our relationship developed over the years, he shared with me his series of books on *The Dallas I Know*, and I read his newspaper on a regular basis. In 2012, I was especially pleased when he decided to donate his papers to the Special Collections Library at the University of Texas at Arlington. It was then that we became good friends and I learned about the many contributions that he has made to the Dallas community that make his autobiography one that all of us should read.

W. Marvin Dulaney
Department of History
UT Arlington

MY LIFE:
THE STORY OF WILLIAM BLAIR

IT WAS BRUTALLY COLD ON THE last Wednesday night in November of 1920 as nine year old William Blair Jr. tried to sleep in the small metal bed that he had shared with his sister, Susie, who was one year older than her only brother.

He and Susie had shared the same bed since the last night that William slept with his parents, William Sr. and Bessie, in the home that they owned located at 2103 N. Washington Street in the northern section of Dallas. Each winter night they pulled themselves under the covers after saying a prayer that their mother had taught them.

Once during the night, William, who was named for his father, had managed to drift off into unconsciousness but the bitter cold of winter gripped his body as if it was an unrelenting vice that would not release his small brown body.

And without warning the urge to empty his bladder confronted him. Yet, the house was bitterly cold and the walk from his bedroom to the bathroom was fearsome. William crossed his legs, tightening them at his thighs in an effort to stop the flow of water. Soon, it was pointless.

The water came rushing from his small penis like a wave in the Pacific Ocean. In a matter of seconds both of his legs, his pajama bottoms and his feet were wet. He lowered his left hand to his knee only to discover that the mattress that he shared with Susie was soaked. While his body was relieved, his heart raced with fear.

My sister is going to wake up and start gasping for air, he whispered. He had relieved himself so fully that he thought the water had drowned her. And now he would have to explain to his mother, who checked their room each morning, Susie's death and a water soaked bed. It was a dreadful situation for young William. He knew that his mother, who changed the sheets on the bed once a week, would be disturbed and he might even get a whipping.

It was something that he did not want to confront. During the remainder of the night he did not sleep. He remained in the bed thinking of explanations that he would give to his mother, all the while praying that the morning sun would find the bed completely dry.

It was too cold to get out of bed and he was afraid that any movement would wake his newly drenched sleeping sister. He watched each movement of her body as she breathed and tossed from one side of the bed to the other during the night which seemed to William the longest that he had ever experienced.

The dawn brought with its rays of sunlight that engulfed the room where William and Susie slept. Now his heart was racing and his feet began to itch as they often did when he was nervous and fearful.

A sense of shock captured him when his mother opened the door to the room, calling both of her children's names as she said 'good morning.' Immediately, like a slice of over toasted bread, Susie jumped from the bed. Her pajamas were wet and her feet were cold.

"Who in the name of my God wet the bed," Mrs. Blair asked with a tinge of anger. "Susie did," William suddenly said while pointing directly at his sister who was still half asleep. "I woke up this morning and my side of the bed was completely wet. It must have happened during the middle of the night," he said convincingly.

Mrs. Blair looked at her daughter with a sense of surprise and disappointment. She had taught her children to go to the bathroom before they went to bed, to empty their bowels in an effort to avoid what had occurred.

"Young lady," she said. "I am disappointed in you because you know better and now I will have to wash the sheets. What kind of example are you setting for your brother?" You would be extremely upset if he had wet the bed," she said as William nodded his head in agreement.

"But I ....."

"Just be quiet, young lady," Mrs. Blair said. "I am going to speak with your father and we will decide what type of punishment you will receive. This is not something that we expect from you. Your father works much too hard for this sort of thing to occur," she said as she was about to leave the room. "We want you to set an example for your brother. Not be a bad influence."

Still bewildered and not fully awake, Susie stood next to the bed rubbing her eyes. William decided that he would rub his eyes as well. She felt her side of the bed as she began to gather the soiled bedding. She rubbed her hands over her pajama bottoms and looked curiously at her brother as if she wanted to say something.

Susie could not remember wetting the bed. But not all doubt escaped her. Perhaps she had an accident during her sleep, she thought to herself, even though it had not happened previously. There was always a first time. She could not remember going to the bathroom before going to bed.

"I can help you carry the sheets to the bathroom," William said to his still bewildered sister. "No, I can do that," she said to William who seemed to have convinced himself that Susie was indeed the culprit of the unwanted late night watering.

"You can go back to bed," she said. "We have got school in few minutes I am going to go help momma clean things up," said Susie who helped their mother with chores about the house.

Quickly, William ran to the bathroom where he took off his undergarments and washed himself with his brown cloth. Later in the morning as he sat across the breakfast table from Susie a sense of shame consumed him. He nearly confessed to his mother but he knew that coming clean would bring a barrage of hardships, including an unrelenting tail whipping from his father who had taught his children to always be truthful.

William and Susie always walked to school together. She was proud of her brother who was popular among his classmates. She took some delight in being related to him. Most mornings they left the yellow wooden frame house where they lived and joyously trekked to learn.

This morning, Susie was still preoccupied with how she had managed to wet the bed. It was most unlike her, but the last thing on her mind was that William was the culprit, and she knew that he would not be untruthful with their parents, particularly their father, who worked as a crew boss in a Planter's oil mill.

School was a five minute walk from their home. This morning they walked briskly because of the harshness of the cold. When they arrived Susie told William that she would see him at the conclusion of the school day and wished him a successful day of learning. Still feeling badly, he nodded and went off with his friends who he met at the school door.

THE BLAIR FAMILY LIVED IN AN integrated neighborhood where children of various races played together although their parents did not mingle as much. Many of the residents owned their homes and some, like the Blair family, even had telephones.

William, who quickly became known as brother to his friends and family was born in the family home. His maternal grandmother, Susie Ross, was the mid-wife who helped to bring him into the world.

Men like the elder Mr. Blair spent most of their time working, believing that their principal duty in life was to provide for these spouses and children. He did not say very much, but he once told his children....."My job is to earn a living and your job is to mind your mother.

There were rigid lines of decorum in the Blair household that were not to be crossed by the children. Violating them meant a harsh whipping, one that made imprints on the body and on the mind.

Many families in the neighborhood bathed once a week. Mr. and Mrs. Blair insisted that their children bath daily. Each member of the family had their personal washing rag and towel that hung on the bathroom door.

In the center of the bathroom was a white bathtub that remained spotless because after each bath it was cleaned by the person who used it. William warmed his bath water on the kitchen stove, poured it into the tub, lathered his body and then jumped into the tub.

Sometimes he soaked for ten or fifteen minutes rubbing and scrubbing, scrubbing and rubbing over every inch of his body. As a very young boy he had a penchant for cleanliness that he learned from his parents and his sister.

After taking his bath, he had to place the green bar of Palmolive in the dish that was beside the tub, empty it and wash away every bit of dirt and grime that had emerged from his body.

The Blair household was many things. It was loving, compassionate and wonderfully strong, but it was not a democracy. Mr. Blair made that abundantly clear. The children did what they were told to do without doubt, disagreement or refusal.

William was told that his job was to be a good student. He was not forced to work to earn extra money to support the family like some children had to do. He was expected to keep his room clean and his clothes in order.

Once every two weeks during the winter months, his mother gave him enough money to purchase a cord of wood from Mr. Willie who drove through north Dallas neighborhoods in a truck selling wood for $150.00 a bundle. William chopped the wood and placed it on the porch, making sure that there was enough to keep the house warm.

On Saturdays, William walked to the mill office that employed his father to pick-up the thirteen dollars that Mr. Blair earned each week. After receiving the money he walked to the grocery store to purchase items on a list that his mother had given to him. After doing the family's shopping he returned home and gave his mother the remainder of his father's pay.

Each evening, the family ate dinner together. Mrs. Blair was a wonderful cook who taught Susie the art of culinary distinction. One evening at dinner, frustrated that she could not get William to chop sufficient pieces of wood, Mrs. Blair informed her husband. Before Mr. Blair could utter a single sound, William blurted out...."You people make me sick."

The room immediately went silent and Mr. Blair stood up from his seat, reached over grabbed his only son by his shirt collar and began a whipping that even the heavyweight prize fighter, Joe Louis, would have admired.

Each time that he struck his eleven year old son's bottom with his massive right hand, Mr. Blair proclaimed...."I walk too hard for you to act like this." After the third blow, William began to cry. The whipping continued. Screams from his mother saved him from having to be taken to the local hospital emergency room.

Mr. Blair listened to the pleading of his wife and lovingly dropped his son to the floor. He took his seat and resumed eating as William rushed to the bathroom to find a jar of Vaseline that he whipped over his butt to sooth the burning.

At the end of the school day, Susie and William dashed home to play with their friends. For the most part, the boys played cowboys while the girls combed the hair of dolls that their parents had purchased.

Mr. Blair and his wife were not regular church goers, but they insisted that their son and daughter be in church each Sunday. So, on the Christian Sabbath day, William and Susie, dressed in their finest clothes, left their home and their parents early enough to be on time for Sunday School at the Munger Avenue Baptist Church which started at 8.30 am.

After Sunday school they sat and listened as the minister preached his message the during morning worship. They left church at noon for lunch at home, returning shortly after eating dinner to participate in the Baptist Young People's Union that was taught by a neighbor. Church was an all day affair.

They grew tired going to church Sunday after Sunday and spending most of the day there, but they dared not to raise any objections with their parents who believed that children should be seen and hot heard and that the Sunday school lessons and preacher's sermon were of value to their children.

William, from time to time, thought of skipping out on church, but was afraid that someone would tell his parents about his absence and that he would have to face the fearsome wrath of his father and his massive right hand.

William was good at playing sporting games; his favorites were football and baseball. He also liked to play marbles. He and his best friend, Charles Brown, who lived a few houses down the block, won so many marbles from other little boys that they began a collection that included marbles of several sizes and colors. They amassed one of largest marble collections in north Dallas and carried them in a small brown bag wherever they traveled in the city.

His ability did not come from skills his father had taught him. He learned on his own. One Christmas, when he was nine years old, his parents purchased him a pair of skates. It was the custom of the Blair children to open their gifts at 2 am in the morning.

He ripped open the box that contained the skates, fastened them to his shoes and rushed to the darkened sidewalk. There was a series of crashes and falls but two hours later he was maneuvering down the sidewalk as if the skates were a permanent attachment to his feet. Learning new things came easy to him. They always did.

Two years later for Christmas, the Blair family sought credit and purchased their son a fashionable western flyer bicycle. It was red and very fast. The only other young boy who received one that Christmas was William's friend, Charles, whose father was an executive with the Excelsior Life Insurance Company, a multi-million dollar operation owned and operated by a group of Black business owners.

The two of them raced their bikes through the neighborhood like two wild stallions. They challenged cars, pedestrians, dogs, cats and anything else that ventured into or near their paths.

Charles and William were together each day. After school they congregated on a corner and decided which city park they would venture to, challenging boys their age and sometimes older, to games of football and baseball.

They were inseparable; wearing the same clothes to school they looked as if they dressed together. The two of them earned money by delivering newspaper to the homes of area residents seven days a week. They worked for the Dallas Morning News and the Express, a weekly newspaper that was owned by a black entrepreneur.

They spent most of their money on clothes and their friends who did not have incomes. Both were very generous. William, unlike Charles, who was from a household of privilege, gave some of his earnings each week to his mother to help with household expenses. It was not something that was requested. It was something that William felt that he should do.

William was a frequent guest, invited and often not, in the Brown household where Charles' mother smothered pork chops and cooked greens that tasted like cotton candy.

Like William in his home, Charles had duties that his parents insisted that he perform before he left for school and after he returned home. The Browns had a sparkling black automobile manufactured by the Ford automobile company, and Charles nor were his sisters never without money.

Mr. Brown, a stately well educated man, treated William as if he were his second son. If Mr. Brown went on a business trip and purchased something special for Charles he would do the same for William. He saw the special bond between the two boys, nurtured it and was hopeful that they would remain life-long friends.

Charles and William séemed to live an idyllic life. Yet, things changed drastically when Mr. Brown died suddenly, leaving a void in the lives of his wife and children.

He had been their anchor and a source of rectitude. His courtliness was such that small boys like William and others emulated him. Some of them walked as he walked, and spoke in the same tone that he used while he was speaking. He was a pillar of the community.

Charles and William were both eleven years old when Mr. Brown died. William rode in the family car with the Brown family to the church and cemetery to eulogize and bury their husband and father. During the ride Charles and William did not speak. They looked straight ahead, knowing that their lives had changed drastically.

Mr. Brown had left a late model black Ford automobile to his family. Years earlier he had taught his son how to drive. His wife and his daughters had never been behind the steering wheel of an automobile. Days after the funeral, Charles and William were driving around town in the car, running errands for Mrs. Brown and taking her place where she needed to go.

Gas station attendants were surprised to see Charles emerge from the driver's seat, pull a wad of money from his pocket, telling them to fill up the car, check the oil and wash the windows.

Charles and Williams cared for each other like brothers. While Charles was from a family of means, well educated and urban, he did not let that stand in the way of his fondness for his friend, William, who father was a member of the working class and whose mother was a housewife.

Charles felt at home in the Blair home, sometimes more so than he did in his own home. The two of them often shared the money that they made from their paper routes. On pay day, they ran to town to shop at the clothing store. Charles usually had more money than William who often gave money to his mother to help pay for groceries and other items around the house.

Once when they went shopping Charles saw a fashionable sweater that caught his fancy. His purchased it with the money that he had brought with him. William wanted the same sweater but he was on a budget and could not afford it.

On the way home, Charles thought about how stylish

he would look in his new sweater and how it would attract the attention of the young school girls. William smiled with his friend but inside he was hurting because he wanted a sweater exactly the same color and style that his friend had purchased, but could not afford it.

When Charles dropped William off at his home he noticed that his friend was not smiling. He asked what was the matter and William answer that he had a headache, but Charles knew better.

When he got home he went into the sock where he kept his money and placed enough money in his pocket to go shopping again the next day. This time, he went without William. Charles went to the same store where he purchased his sweater, the one that his friend liked so much.

The salesperson recognized him and thought for a moment that he wanted to return the item. When he told him that he wanted a second sweater, the same color and same size, he was thrilled.

He even offered to wrap it for him but Charles asked that it simply be placed in a bag and he left the store. He drove straight to William's house and called for his friend to come to the front porch. When William came outside he noticed that Charles was wearing the sweater that he liked so much and wished that he had.

"I have something for you," Charles said as he handed the bag over to William. "What is it?"

"Just look inside," Charles said.

William's face brightened as he pulled the sweater from the bag. He could smell its freshness and immediately pulled it over his head and stroked his hands down its front.

"You did not have to do this for me," he said.

"Yes, I did," said Charles. "Let's go for a ride in the car. Make sure you wear your sweater."

"You think I am going to take if off. No way, man," William said. "I am going to sleep in this thing tonight. They might even have to bury me in it one day."

One of the reasons that Charles and William got along so well was that they both had dreams. Charles often talked of following his father in business. Maybe one day he would be a banker or own his own company, he told William.

Unlike Charles, William did not know exactly what he wanted to do with his life. He was proud of the work that his father did at the mill but he saw himself in a suit and tie. He did not want to do manual labor. I want to work with my mind, he told Charles one day as they walked from their paper routes.

His first seven years of schooling were spent at BF Darrell, an elementary school known for quality instructors and great discipline. It was in a large building, three stories high and it had seven hundred students.

William was excited being a student. He liked walking to school. His first role model was Odis Owens, a boy scout, who directed younger students in the morning and at the end of the school day as they crossed the streets around the school.

He liked it most when Odis barked out orders to other students in his loud and commanding voice. "Don't cross there," he yelled. "Stop, can't you see my hand in front of you."

William told Charles that he wanted to be like Odis, someday in charge of other students and telling them when they could move and when they had to stand still. "I like the way that he handles things," William said.

The very first teacher that William remembers at Darrell was Maureen Bailey who later became a great choir director at Lincoln High School. Like most of the female teachers at the school, Ms. Bailey lived in the neighborhood and treated everyone with respect and decorum.

His favorite teacher in elementary school, however, was L.R. Lockhart. He was a disciplinarian who taught the seventh grade. No one talked or passed notes in his class. He was six feet two inches tall, weighed nearly 240 pounds and was the closest thing to God that William had ever experienced, including some of the preachers that he knew. No one talked or chewed gun during Mr. Lockhart's classes. Even if they were not interested they acted as though they were because Lockhart did not have problem with pummeling a behind or cracking a set of knuckles.

Teachers like Mr. Lockhart lived to educate the young minds who were their wards for most of the day while their parents earned a living. They wanted to see boys like William do better than their parents. After all, they had more opportunity and were further removed from slavery. They did not want to see their students grow up to pick cotton in the harsh Texas sun.

William did not like school. He went because his parents insisted that he attend and because his best friend, Charles, said that it was something that young men like the two of them had to do. There was one advantage to being in school, girls, and William grew fond of them.

Teachers like Mr. Lockhart and Ms. Marshall were members of the same churches as their students and they lived in the same neighbrohood. If ever William misbehaved at school his teacher would stop at his home on his or her way home. After telling Mr. and Mrs. Blair what William had done or had not done, he knew it was time to get the strap.

The whippings were so harsh in the Blair household that William made a point of obeying his teachers. Once he hooked school with a group of friends. To his shock his principal came to his home and told his parents that he had not seen their son at school. He received a whipping at home and a second one the next morning at school after he was called to the office by the principal.

Students studied for four days when William was an elementary school student. On Fridays the schools held assemblies where students were taught current events and good graces. Friday was also designated as classical music day. The idea was that students had to be cultured in order to survive the world. William and each of his schoolmates had to learn to sing the Negro National Anthem. They were taught that it was a proud song, sung by a proud people. The teachers taught William and other students the history behind the song.

He did not understand why some of his teachers cried when they sang the song or why it was that the older students stood erect as the words rolled through their lips. In years to come he would understand the tears and the seriousness with which those who sang the song demonstrated.

William always found himself among the smallest boys in his class, if not the smallest. He was constantly challenged by other boys because of his size. At times he tried to get recognition by being loud and showing off in class.

He decided that he would not back down and that the only way they he could make up for his shortness of stature was to be bold in his personality. So, if someone yelled at him he returned the yell, but louder. If someone called him a name he fixed his lips and called them the worst thing that he had ever heard uttered by an adult.

In the beginning he fought nearly every day, having been picked on by larger boys in the morning and in the afternoon. He did not like fighting but soon became good at it. Before long the larger boys left him alone. By then he had a reputation as a fierce and determined fighter who would rather be beaten into the ground than to give up. From time to time his sister, Susie, joined in fights with him. It was not long before it became known that if you picked on one Blair you had to fight two of them.

Williams' reputation as a fighter grew. He liked o fight at the YMCA and for years he beat anyone who dared to step into the ring with him. Charles was his boxing assistant. He sat outside the ropes and wiped his face and back between rounds and made sure that he had plenty of water to drink.

Their roles as boxer and assistant helped them to attract girls and soon other youngsters began to call William champ. He liked the sound of the title and began to brag about his abilities. He talked so much that one of the older man in the gym named him radio.

His reign as champion came to an end when he stepped into the ring to fight one of the school's better boxers. William often paid more attention to the girls sitting near the front of the ring than he did to his opponents. He underestimated his opponent who hit him harder than anyone had ever hit him. A teacher, who was also a sports writer, laughed as William was knocked from one side of the ring to the other. William called for Charles to throw in the towel which he did to keep his friend from being killed.

William acquired his first girl friend, Bernice Atkins, when he was in elementary school. They were in the same class. She had come to Dallas from Cleburne, Texas with her family and he liked her because she had smooth brown skin and plump brown legs.

Bernice wore her hair split down the middle. She talked with William but he did not know whether or not she felt that same affection that he felt for her. He decided that he would attract her attention by walking pass her house. One day he walked pass her house seven times. He did that several days until she finally opened the doors and came to the porch.

He told her that he would walk to her house before going to school and that he would carry her books if she walked with him. She said that she liked the idea. So, each morning he walked to Bernice's house, took her books from her while her mother watched from inside the house and the two of them walked to school. At the end of the school day he walked her home and placed her books on her porch. He was not allowed to go inside and he was not allowed to kiss her. But he felt as though he was in love and walking with her and carrying her books was enough to keep his heart pounding.

At home William had chores, some that he shared with his sister. Three times each week it was his turn to wash dishes. Once a week he cut wood for the stove that kept the house warm in winter.

On one occasion he neglected to chop the wood as his mother had requested. At dinner that evening she told her husband that William had refused to chop the wood that the family needed. William said something smart to his father.

Just as he nearly completed his last sentence, Mr. Blair commenced the whipping. It was so severe that Mrs. Blair demanded that he stop. William limped into his room to ease his behind.

The senior Mr. Blair was a very proud man who worked hard to support his wife and two children. Six days each week he toiled to support them. He asked very little of his children, but insisted that they do their school work and that they were obedient to their parents. When they were not, he felt that they were ungrateful, something that he would not accept.

Unlike her brother, Susie was a loner who spent much of her idle time in the company of her mother rather than with other girls her age. She had a mean streak that she displayed if somewhat crossed her. She was extremely loyal to her father, her mother and brother.

Around the various neighbrohoods in the Dallas, William developed a reputation for being a good athlete. He best sports were football and baseball. White baseball players, a few years older than William, always wanted him to play on their teams and despite his size; he was among the first chosen to play on football teams.

Unlike many young boys, he and Charles had extra money so they could afford to purchase equipment. With ownership came the ability to set the rules. Charles and William went from neighborhood to neighborhood with their equipment. If a game toured sour they would often gather their balls and call an end to the games. They both like the ability to determine when a game was finished. Often they laughed as they role home, having called a game early because they disputed a play.

When it came time to go to high school, William decided that he would attend Booker T. Washington, a football powerhouse which was named after the legendary founder of Tuskeegee Institute in Alabama. The school's main rival was Lincoln which was named after the President whose work led to the abolition of chattel slavery.

Still small in stature, William was known for his heart, his shifting running skills and his hard hitting ability as a defensive player. R.E. Fields and Raymond Holley, the head and assistant football coach, liked his style of play and took a special interest in William.

Holley had a reputation of being one of the best teachers of fundamentals in the city of Dallas. He taught young men, who were willing, how to take a little talent and become giants on the football field. William listened to every word that he said in practice.

Unlike the academic side of school, William enjoyed athletics. There were some very good football players on the team during his first year. They all wanted to be champions, and recognized as the very best football players in the state of Texas.

During William's first year the team won six games and lost four. It was an unacceptable record to the young players and their coaches. They knew they could do better and were determined to do so. The practices of the team were long and very tough. The school did not have lights so the coaches turned the headlights of their cars on when darkness came and the players were able to practice into the night.

During the off season, William and his fellow teammates would practice together. Charles was not a football player but supported his friend in his efforts.

William made efforts to gain more weight but for the most part was unsuccessful.

The hard work of the team members paid off. During their second year the team one ten games and lost one but that was not seen as good enough. The goal was to go undefeated.

In his senior year, William's team won the state championship in football. They were undefeated and only gave up a total of twelve points in twelve football games. Williams was a starting halfback whose nickname was peel, because of the style that he wore his hair.

That state championship game was played before 8,000 screaming fans in the Cotton Bowl in Dallas. It was the day before his birthday, October 16th, and he scored the first touchdown, a pass play that went fifty-five years. He could hear Susie screaming her lungs out in the stands. They played their arch-rival, Lincoln.

Mr. and Mrs. Brown, knowing that their son was a star football player, did not watch him play football. They were afraid that he was going to get hurt and did not want to see him injured. Their daughter gave them the gridiron details after each game. They had to wait until she calmed down.

Earning a letter each year that he played in high school made William a rather popular student with his fellow students, particularly the girls. He like the adoration and proudly walked through the halls of the school in his varsity jacket with his football gear in a bag that he carried over his shoulder.

In the classroom he was not a slouch. He simply did not apply himself. He thought that he would one day become a professional baseball or football player and that was enough for him. He did not see where academics would help him.

His grandmother gave him one whipping when he was a small boy. He and his cousin were fighting in her backyard in Ft. Worth. She stepped between them, saving, "Kin folks don't fight."

Close to members of his extend family when he was small, William was particularly fond of his uncle, Diego Ross, who was a talented artist. He also was fond of Thelma Milton, his mother's sister who lived in a small room with the Blair family while her mother raised her son in Ft. Worth.

Thelma worked cleaning houses for whites of means in North Dallas. When she was paid she purchased something special for her son, who she went to visit. She also purchased a gift for her William who grew to worship his quietly diminutive aunt.

William did not know why his aunt lived apart from her son and never asked. Children were "seen but not heard" in the Blair home. They were well respected and their needs were met but their opinions were not solicited. It was the same in other homes in the neighborhood.

On Saturday evenings Mr. Blair made "home brew" for himself and a fellow worker, Mr. Stone, who came by the Blair home. The two of them sat on the front porch or in the kitchen and drank until they could not walk. The two of them were not loud and did not argue. They simply drank and had fun.

There were white neighbors across the state from the Blair one. One family was prominent in the Italian underworld. The father was called Chicken Louie Fantalla. William frequented their home, played with their children and grew fond of spaghetti and meat balls while having meals with them. The children did now acknowledge race and did not call one another names other than their own.

A white woman, who Mrs. Blair did business with, grew to like William and Susie. One day she visited the Blair home and brought two ponies with her for the children. William and Susie were afraid of the animals and kept them for two days before their mother returned them to Ms. McGhee.

The first time William experienced grief was at 13 when his beloved dog, Bessie, was hit and killed by a cab. William was playing in front of his home after school when he saw his dog in the distance. Bessie, who waited for William at the front gate while he was away at school, was running towards him, his tail gently wagging in the air.

The cab driver did not see him and stopped when he hit him. William was shocked. He yelled his dog's name and rushed towards him. When he arrived at the spot of the accident he knew that Bessie was dead. William grabbed his two back legs and pulled him out of the street, afraid that another car would run over his body.

He received permission from his parents to bury Bessie in the backyard. He and Charles held a service, complete with a prayer and buried the dog in a hole that they had dug. On nights, when he could not sleep, William would go into the yard and stand near the grave. On his way to school he paused at the gate where he left Bessie. He hoped that she would be there when he returned from school later in the day.

Williams grieved over Bessie for months. While not a human being, the animal had a place in the young boy's heart. He did not understand why the dog had been killed and often spoke with him before falling off to sleep at night. He once told Charles that he wanted to go the place where his dog has gone, but his friend consoled him and told him that he would be alright.

Charles and William spent a fortune at the local movie theater. They did not pay for admission because the manager, E. G. Bodden, was a neighbor who let the boys in for free. He liked them, particularly their enterprising spirits. Mr. Bodden did not like lazy children and tried his best to keep them away from the theater.

The two of them spent their money impressing girls. Whenever a girl that they liked came to the movie they would offer her popcorn, drinks, candy and whatever else she and her friends wanted. The friends had to be female though.

Charles liked Westerns. After watching the same movie for three or four times he would go home, found an old broom and place it between his legs. His pretended that the stick was his horse and that he was a sheriff riding through the Wild West in search of outlaws.

One Saturday when William and Charles arrived at the movie theater, thinking that they would be watching a diet of westerns, the two of them were quickly moved into shock.

A horror picture was showing. Williams was sitting on the front row and when the monster appeared on the screen it appeared as though he was coming right for him. He nearly wet his pants. Charles covered his face with his hands, but for some reason William was frozen. All he could think to do was cry out for his mother.

The manager, Mr. Bodden, rushed to the front of the theater and tried to quiet William but he would not stop screaming. "I want my mother, I want my mother," he repeated over and over again. Mr. Bodden rushed to his office and called Mrs. Blair who rushed to the movie theater to quiet her young son. She was able to dislodge him from his seat and took him home. It was weeks before he returned to the movies and he never once against watched a horror picture.

In addition to being known as a good athlete and a boy that liked to have fun, William earned a reputation of being somewhat of an artist on the dance floor. He and Charles would often pool their money to rent toe YMCA to have a dance, compete with a dee-jay who played records and encouraged the youngster to show their best stuff on the dance floor.

William was always one of the first on the floor. He quickly mastered the new dance crazes and demonstrates them on the floor of the Y while other young men and their girl friend watched in awe. Each time that he performed he danced like he was in a constant with a $100.00 prize. In his mind there was no reason to believe that he would not be running home with a huge wad of money in his pocket.

William was in fact a very good dancer. So good that others attempted to emulate his moves while he danced with their girlfriends. Those who were brave went out on dance floor and danced with him.

Williams kicked his heels, did splits on the floor and waved his jacket in the air above his head. He was in his element. The Dee-jay that he and Charles paid called out his name and chanted "go Mr. Smooth, go."

As the years of youth went by, William and Charles continued to sell newspapers, sponsored parties at the YMCA, walk their girlfriends to school and home and enjoy life.

Charles taught William to drive the car that his father left him. They enjoyed the one day that Blacks could go the state fair, the Juneteenth celebrations and the opportunities that William had to practice with the pro and semi-pro baseball teams that spent time in Dallas.

Williams, a fairly decent hitter excelled at pitching. He was a southpaw who had an uncanny ability to strikeout batters. Charles was his practice catcher. One day when the two of them were playing catch in the neighborhood, William developed a pitch, with the assistance of his friend.

It was a curve ball that dropped between four and two feet just second before it reached the plate. The boys named the pitched twelve to six. It was unhittable and served William well when he entered the Negro Baseball Leagues as a hard throwing lefty.

THE YOUNG MEN AND WOMEN WHO went to Lincoln went college after high school. Education was valued and it was seen as a pathway to greater success in life. Many of the students who were graduated with William in 1938 attended schools such as Howard University, Fisk University, Wiley College, Paul Quinn, Morgan State University and Prairie View A&M located in South Texas.

William had never gained a knack for academics, but knew that it was expected that he attend an institution of higher learning. He chose Prairie View, located about an hour from Houston. A number of students from Lincoln joined him there in the summer of 1940.

It was only weeks before he decided that he did not fit in. The university was highly structured. Students were expected to attend class and chapel and boys were asked to him their distance from girls. William soon became sullen. He did not like the idea of being far away from a city, did not have a car and had not found a girl that he liked.

William decided that he would leave Prairie View but was not fascinated with the idea of having to convince his mother and his father that he knew what he was doing with his life. He decided that he join the Army, although he was too young to join without the permission of one of his parents.

He knew that they would not go along with the idea. So, he contacted Mrs. Helen Dixon, an administrator at Lincoln and a neighbor. He convinced her to sign his mother's signature on the enlistment papers. On August 16th, armed with the forged papers, he became a member of the United States Army.

His mother, when she learned what her son had done, was not thrilled. His father held another position. "If he wants to be a solider then let him become a soldier," he said to his wife and son.

Assigned to Ft. Sill, Oklahoma, William and twelve other young recruits took a train from downtown Dallas to the Army base. Once in Oklahoma City, they took a bus to the fort. There he joined other Black recruits who were preparing themselves to participate in the War against Adolph Hitler and the Japanese.

Although the Black recruits knew that they would not fight for their country, they were proud to wear the uniform of their country, to march in victory parades and salute the American flag.

Before enlisted into the Army, Blair married his school sweetheart, Mozelle Jordan. She was a high school beauty who fit his two standards, brown skins and pretty round legs.

Mozelle brought stability in his life and he love her very much. Together they had seven children and for a brief period when he played professional baseball she traveled with the team. But her heart was always in Dallas where she wanted to settle down and raise her children and start a catering business.

I had dreamed of playing baseball with icons like Satchel Paige and Josh Gibson. I got my chance when I joined the Negro Baseball League as a young left handed pitcher.

I got my start with the Birmingham Black Barons. When I arrived in that sleepy southern town, a driver picked me up from the railroad station. He looked at my size while he drove me to my hotel and asked me three times if I was Bill Blair. He was looking for a much bigger man with a large arm and trunks for legs.

He did not find that in me. I was small, not six feet tall and weighed less than 150 pounds, but I knew that I could pitch. When I took the mound for the first time and struck out most of the batters that I faced mouths began to drop and I knew that I would one day be a star.

When I went to pitch for the Indianapolis Clowns, Bunny Downs was the business manager. He stood outside of each hotel that we stayed in and addressed everyone who passed with "how are you doing Mr. Lee?"

It did not matter if they were black, brown, white or red. It was always the same, "how are you Mr. Lee?" He stood in front of a hotel for an hour or so, referring to everyone as "Mr. Lee."

Once I approached him and asked why he called everyone Mr. Lee. "Blair, he said, "I am calling them ugly, not Mr. Lee." Downs traveled with the club. He made the sleeping arrangements and paid each of us each Sunday and gave us our eating money, $14.00 for the entire week.

I did pretty well. Goose Tatum, who also played for the Harlem Globetrotters, played first base for our team. He was also my roommate and talked from the first batter in the first inning until the last batter in the ninth. He would say "hum that rock, radio," the name he was fond of calling me.

"You can't hit radio," he yelled to batter after batter. When they struck out, Goose laughed them into the dugout and continued laughing throughout the inning. On the bench he sat next to me and would usually say "you are one damn good pitcher, boy."

While he laughed on the field, Goose was somewhat of a sad man. He drank most nights after our games and even played some games with liquor on his breath. "Blair, don't let them hit you," he would say to me. "You can't let those bums get on base."

Many of the men who played for the Negro baseball league were college educated. They were as good as the white men who played in the Major Leagues and often talked about how they would have done if they were given a chance.

We played games most nights of the week, traveling from city to city, one a bus driver by our catcher, Double Duty, who made extra money for driving the bus. In addition to pitching I also swung a pretty good bat. My favorite was a thirty-two inch Louisville slugger.

The League was started by a former baseball pitcher from Texas named Andrew Rube Foster. A burley man, Rube formed his own team, the Chicago American Giants in 1910. Ten years later he started the Negro League. He guaranteed that players would receive regular paychecks, instituted annual all-star games and demanded that players excel in their chosen sport.

Foster knew that one day the white major leagues would be opened to Black ball players and he gave his wards advice that would allow them to make the transition. It was a tough job, being both an owner and league commissioner.

He played a tough brand of baseball and pushed his players physically. He pushed himself and suffered a nervous breakdown in 1926. In a few years he was dead.

My worse moment in a baseball game came when John Miles, who played for the Chicago American Giants, hit a grand slam against me. We were playing in San Antonio and he hit one of the longest balls I have ever seen sail out of a ballpark.

I watched the ball as it disappeared. He hit it with three balls and two strikes against him. He was looking for a fast ball and I threw him one. I felt like a waiter delivering a meal to a man who had not eaten in two weeks. I had forgotten that he was a power pitcher. My manager did not take me out of the game. In fact, we won the game, but the experience stayed with me the entire time that I played in the league.

The Clowns not only played baseball but we put on a show for our fans, sometimes they numbered as many as 20,000 for a game and we had two objectives, give them a victory and make them laugh.

The team had a midget called Bebob. He would run around the bases and stand in the batter's box. He uniform was too big for him and wore colorful shoes. King Tut was our master showman. He ran into the stands and sat with fans. He threw popcorn at them and even water. He grabbed wigs from the heads of women and sat on the laps of fat people.

He and Goose had a routine, pretending that they were rowing a boat on the mount. King Tut fell out of the boat and Goose dived overboard to save him. Tut would pretend that he drowned and Goose would give him mouth to mouth resuscitation. I often laughed so hard at their antics that I hurt my side when I pitched. I saw them perform every year for six straight years. And I laughed each time they performed.

Each fall stars from the Major Leagues and the Negro Baseball League would play one another in a series of game in California. The Negro League Players often won the games. A few of the white players, such as Ted Williams, urged Major League owners to allow Black players to play on their teams. But their pleas fell on deft ears.

Some of the best hitters in baseball were in the Negro League. They included Josh Gibson, a native of Georgia who played catcher for the Homestead Grays, one of the most feared teams in the Negro Baseball League.

Gibson was so strong that he once hit a home run that was measured at 550 feet. He played the entire year and seldom average less than 350. His lifetime average was nearly 400 and but for segregation he would have been a bigger star than Babe Ruth.

Gibson was a fearsome hitter, but I learned that you could only get him out if you were not afraid of him. You had to ignore the legend. If you did not you were finished. The few times that I pitched against him I did well. Gibson had a habit of rolling up his left sleeve and hitting home plate with bat before the first pitch was thrown to him.

Many a pitcher nearly had a heart attack while facing Gibson who was later elected to the baseball hall of fame

There were many fans that came to games who did not like baseball but they liked to see a show and did Goose and King Tut ever give them a show.

Tut was the life of the team. He was in the league for many years and was one of the sharpest dressers I have ever seen. He liked to drink, play dice and chase women. After his baseball career he traveled from city to city. He never settled down and ended up in an insane asylum.

During our bus trips most of the players sang songs and played card games. A few of us read newspapers. I read every newspaper that I could get my hands on. Only the Black Press, such as the Baltimore Afro American and the Pittsburg Courier, carried stories on Black baseball. If you wanted to read our exploits you had to read them in one the papers targeted to African Americans. The white papers, for the most part, treated us as though we did not exist.

My best friend on the Clowns was Sherwood Brewer. We had started in baseball together and we hit it off the very first time that we met. A fine infielder, Brewer was from Clarksdale, Mississippi. He was a finesse baseball player who hit any pitch close to the plate out of the ballpark.

On the road, when we were not practicing , Brewer and I went to the entertainment districts. We both liked to dance. My friend was a short man and weighed about 160 pounds. He liked to fight and did not have much to say. I felt safe with him because he handled himself like a middle weight boxer.

One of the greatest pitchers to ever hold a baseball in his hand was Leroy "Satchel" Paige who was born July

7th in Mobile, Alabama. I saw Satchel pitch and instruct all of his outfielders to sit down.

I first met Satchel Paige in 1940. I had never seen anyone pitch like him. When he threw the ball you shut your eyes and imagined that bacon was cooking. Crowds came to the ballpark to see Satchel perform. They knew that they were seeing a magician at work.

During his career, he pitched more than 2500 games with one hundred or more being no hitters. In 1930, against a team of white major leaguers, Satchel struck out twenty-two batters. His fast ball was called the "bee-ball" because it buzzed when he threw it. His wondrous "hesitation pitch" was evil that it was declared illegal by league officials.

Famous for his condition, Satchel pitched excelled as a pitcher until he was nearly sixty years old. During one season, Satchel pitched in more than 150 games. Sometimes he would pitch every day for seven straight days. He won more than 2000 games.

I once saw him ask his outfielders to sit down while he pitched to the hardest part of another team's lineup. He was unafraid and daring. None of us knew his real age. We assumed that he was a few years older than most of us. We respected him tremendously so no one asked.

Satchel's best pitch was his fastball, but he had a wicked curb ball and a nasty slider. He often kicked his left leg higher than his head and I thought he would fall down before he released the ball.

Durable as a bull, Satchel pitched complete games, sometimes twice a day. There was no such thing as a relief pitcher and pitches like me and Satchel also had to bat. We stood in the batter's book and took our cuts just everybody else.

During the height of segregated baseball, white

scouts came to see Satchel pitch. Some of them, thinking that the separation was stupid, desperately wanted to sign Satchel. Even established baseball players in the white league, like Ted Williams, wanted to see Sat cell signed by a white club.

Fans came to see us play in the thousands. Sometimes we played two games in one day. Our catcher, Leonard Pigg, was also our bus driver and he often drove from ballpark to ballpark with his uniform on. He did not mind because he got extra pay.

The Negro League was laced with great athletes. "Double Duty" Radcliffe, another native of Mobile, Alabama was in such great shape that he often pitched the first game in a double header and was behind the plate during the second game on the same day.

He did this for nearly twenty-two years with twelve different ball clubs. More than five times Double Duty was named to the all-star team. He was a thinker behind the plate and a wise sage on the mound. He was well liked and later became a manager.

Most of the players in the Negro League were college graduated. They came from some of the best Black colleges in the country and made more money playing baseball than they could have working a profession where they would not have been able to fully utilize the skills that they had learned in college.

Among the best players were the Cubans. They could hit the ball a mile and boy could they pitch. One of the pitchers who taught me hold to hold players on base was Luis Tiant. You had to be a fool to attempt to steal a base on him. He started his pitching motion with both of his hands in his glove at eye level. He then slowly lowered his globe and watched the runner at the same time.

I once saw a ball player nearly faint because he thought that Tiant was going to throw him out. He had taken a lead from the base and felt a pain in his leg. He knew that if Tiant throw to the first baseman he would be thrown out. Instead of getting picked off, he called for time and saved himself the embarrassment.

The Cuban players, even the ones who looked like whites, did not believe in racism. They saw everyone as a human being. That's what was so special about them. They treated everyone fairly.

The only thing I did not like about them was when they started talking in Spanish. "Shut the hell up and speak English," Goose would say from time to time. They knew he was playing and continued to speak in their native tongue.

They were very proud people and did not believe in your making fun of their country. They did not get along that well with the players from the Dominican Republic. I thought because they all spoke Spanish they would get along but that was not the case. Some of the Cubans were closer to the Blacks than they were to the Dominicans.

The Clowns were a team that believed in giving people a show. We sent midgets to the plate and set off firecrackers under the stands. The ownership of the team wanted the fans to have a good time. Entire families came to the ballpark. The men came in suits and the women wore lovely dresses.

One of the things that I liked doing was signing autographs. Especially the author graphs for young pretty women who came to see us play. Some of my teammates often made bets about who had the most girl friends in the cities where we played.

On the team bus most of the players slept. There

was a group that played cards. They sat in the middle of the bus while the group that shot crap sat in the rear. I usually sat towards the front of the bus where I could read a newspaper. Sometimes Goose sat with me and other times I sat alone.

Whenever we traveled to a different city I bought the newspaper. It was a way to learn about the culture of the town. In Biltmore I read the Afro-Americans Newspaper which was owned by the Murphy family. Their sports rider, Sam Lacy, covered the Negro Baseball League and was one of the most honorable men I had ever met.

He was one hell of the writer and was a stickler for details. If you wanted to know what really went on during a game you had to read Sam Lacy's columns. He advocated Blacks going to the white major leagues

Another paper that I read was the Pittsburg Courier. I got it whenever we went there to play the Grays. Their sports writer, Jackie, like Mr. Lacy was an advocate for Negro Baseball players. He often wrote about how long we hit the ball and how good our pitchers were.

Whenever the Negro League All-stars beat the white all-stars, the Pittsburg paper carried the results of the game on the front page. It was their way of participating in the civil rights movement.

The white newspapers did a disservice to the Black community, I believed. In Dallas 1947, a black worker, Travis Lee, was shot and killed in front of the Harlem Theater by a white police officer by the name of Gus Edwards.

The leading white daily carried a two paragraph story about the shooting. The paper seldom covered the Black community and for the most part ignored it.

On the road my social companion was called Sparky.

He as in infielder from the Deep South. He was a sharp dresser and he liked to fight. As soon as we hit a town we asked the bell hops at the hotels where the hot spots were located and off we went. I liked him because he was a sober man, but he flew off the handle after a few drinks. I saw him beat a man close to death one night in Midwestern town. He was arrested because he was a member of a professional baseball team and the police who responded liked baseball

One of the officers asked for his autograph and wanted to know if we could get him tickets to the game. We told him to stop by the ticket officer the next day. When he got there his tickets were waiting for along with two autographed baseballs, one for him and the other for his brother.

Whorehouses and clothing stores made a lot of money during the baseball season. Most of the players liked women and nearly all of my teammates like to dress well. We had one player called "Jetson" who had a different suit for every day of the week. He was always color coordinated with even his socks matching his shirt and his handkerchief.

Now, on the ball field he stayed dirty, sliding into base and diving for balls but once the game was over he headed straight to his suitcase and spent about an hour trying to decide what he would wear to the local club.

Some of the ballplayers sang spirituals during our long bus rides. The Clowns had two or three quartets. On Sundays, before the game, they sought out a local church. When the minister discovered who they were, they volunteered that they were gospel singers who lived the Lord.

Because we played during segregation none of the

white newspapers carried news of our achievements. What I did on a weekly basis was not known by the average citizen in Dallas because it was not in the local newspaper. Even though white reporters came to some of our games, they could not write about what they had witnesses. Their editors would simply ignore it.

One time when I everything I threw was being hit out of the park, the manager came to the mound and told me to go take a shower. I told him that I had "more gas in my tank." He said that I should use that gas to fart and that I needed to get to the dugout as quickly as possible. "you're stinking up the place," he said.

I was a very proud pitcher and I knew I was getting killed but I thought I could turn things around. I had just beaten the team we were playing by five runs four days earlier. Surely they could not continue to trash me, I said.

My manager was not going for it so he reached for the ball. I placed my glove behind my back and he reached for it. He tussled for about two minutes before Goose came to the mound and said "radio….. I think you need to take a seat." He then gave me a little pat on my butt.

We were playing in a stadium in Little Rock, Arkansas and the stands were nearly full. I felt foolish and was embarrassed. Just as I was leaving, the second baseman, Riddles, yelled "get out of here before you get one of us killed. Goose smiled at me as I crossed the white chalk line.

For the rest of the game I sat on the bench nearly crying. I knew I could beat this team. I had just beaten them. I was twenty-four years old and did not believe in failure. I thought I had been treated unfairly and refused to go to the shower. I rode back to the hotel in my baseball uniform. When I got to the room I took off my clothes, had a hot bath and went to bed. Goose was out drinking, shooting crap or pursuing some young woman.

The only player to hit a gram slam against me was John Miles who played with the Chicago American Giants. We were playing in San Antonio. For most of the day I handled him very well when he came up to bat. This time he pushed me to a three balls, two strikes count. I decided to throw a pitch that would hit the plate but also come close to hitting hit since he leaned over in the batter's box.

Miles started to smile as the curve I threw was coming towards him. It was as if he had ordered the pitch just like he ordered his lunch. He was a power hitter and I heard the sound of the bat crashing up against the cowhide that covered the baseball.

I immediately lowered my head as his teammates stared to yell and laugh as they rounded the bases. Those in the dugout ran towards home plate to create a welcoming party for him.

Miles did not say anything or even look my way as he covered the three bases and then home plate. In was the first time in the fifteen years that I had been playing the game that anyone hit a grand slam against me. I was disgusted and embarrassed and wanted to go home.

My favorite catcher was a charming individual called Sambo Hariston who was born in Birmingham, Alabama. He was there when I arrived in Indianapolis and was an important part of the team. He knew the type of game I liked to pitch and called a good game. He did not gamble with my pitches and took his time calling a game.

We did not have trainers in the Negro League and sometimes a pitcher was on the mound times a week. There were double headers where I pitched in the first game and in the second game. If something hurt your arm you took some aspirin. Some of the older pitches had personal home remedies, usually concoctions that they rubbed on their arms and their feet.

There was not much sympathy for an injured player in the league. We viewed ourselves as soldiers and each game was a war. If you were injured you were carried to the side and left there. No one cured you or cried for you. That is just the way it was. Each of us knew if we got hurt we would lose our jobs so we just played through the pain. The pay was good in Negro baseball.

When Jackie Robinson, who played in the Negro Baseball League, was called up to Major League Baseball we were very happy for him. But we knew that there were much better players than Jackie. He had the right temperament and would not react with anger.

In fact, we knew that we could field a team that was much better, position for position, than any of the teams in the white leagues. Players seldom talked about it but we knew that we were among the best baseball players in the world. And we had the stats to prove it.

When the baseball season was over a number of players in the Negro Baseball League went to Mexico, Central American and South America to play baseball in leagues there. I was asked to go to the Dominican Republic more than once but I was afraid of flying and decided to stay home. At the end of each season I returned to Dallas to be with my family and accept the role of a local hero.

While I was not an all-star pitcher I held my own. My reputation was that I was one of the league's best lefties, pitching well to right handed and left handed batters. I did not pitch around any batters and I enjoyed a challenge.

When it came to hitting, I can best be described as a "sprayer." I hit the ball to a number of fields and outfielders could not sit in a single position when I came to the plate. I hit solid line drives and on more than once occasion helped my team win very tight ball games.

My fast ball, curve, change up and twelve to six pitch served me well throughout my career. I had five good years and during the months before my sixth year in 1949 I began to prepared myself, as I had each year, for spring training.

At camp I visited with my old friends and introduced myself to the rookies. There was always tremendous talent that wanted to get into the league. I remained in shape by remembering the lessons taught to me by Raymond Hollie, who coached football at Booker T. Washington High School in Dallas.

Coach Hollie was born in Calvert, Texas. Graduated from Bishop College he became at coach at Booker T. Washington in 1939. He coached championship teams and placed an emphasis on staying in shape. "Treat your bodies like they are temples," he yelled at his players, including me. Coach Hollie, called the Old Joker, challenged athletes to give everything they have on the field and off."

That is the philosophy I adopted while playing in the Negro Leagues. Lay everything on the line and give one hundred percent each and every play which is what coach Hollie taught me and the hundreds of young athletes that he trained and who came to adore him. I knew that sometimes I faced stronger pitchers and hitters but they did not have inside of them what I had inside of me. It was planted years ago on the field at Booker T. Washington by men like Coach Hollie.

Baseball practice was always very tough. We ran laps and did calisthenics. We worked from sunrise to sundown and we played baseball like young boys who encountered the game for the first time. Each of us knew that playing in the Negro League was an honor that was not to be taken lightly and I did not.

The season started like the others did. I pitched for a few innings during games of spring training, fielded ground balls and took batting practice. The first game of the season that I pitched I felt pain in my arm and then I felt nothing. It was as if I was throwing a rubber band rather than a baseball. On a few pitches, the ball hit the dirt well before the plate. The Seattle fans near the dugout made crude jokes as I stepped off the field.

I looked over at the dugout and saw a worried look on the face of our manager, Buster Haywood. He could see the pain in my face which I was to conceal. When I came to the bench at the end of the first inning he asked me if something was wrong. I told him that I was fine.

When I went out for the second inning the pain had intensified. I wanted to keep my job and kept my mouth shut. I bit my lip when I threw the first pitch and it hit the dirt three feet in front of the plate. The second was no better. Goose ran to the mound, joined by the other infielders.

"What's going on, Radio," Goose asked.

"Not a damn thing," I said.

C'mon. Hum that rock," Goose said as he patted me on my right shoulder and ran back towards first base.

The very next pitch hit the dirk, way short of the first. I turned to look at Haywood who was sprinting towards the mound. When he reached me he grabbed the ball and told me go to take a shower.

Without protest I ran from the mound into the dugout and spent the rest of the night popping aspirin and anything else I could to deaden the pain. When Goose came to the room I was asleep. He did not wake me and was very quiet that night.

The next morning I rushed to the ball field before other players reported to practice. I tried throwing a baseball into a net. Each time I threw the ball, my arm hurt. I knew that there was something wrong but did not know quite what to do.

I asked Haywood for his advice and he suggested that I return to Dallas, rest the army for a few weeks and then return to the team. He pledged that I would have a job when I returned. I took his advice and caught a train home.

I found a doctor in Dallas who examined my arm. He gave me a cream and told me to rub it every four hours. It deadened the pain but it did not feel like it had before. Two weeks later I joined the team in Denver.

During the time that I was away Goose roomed by himself. On the very first night I was back he asked me if I was sure that I could handle the rock.

"What the hell else am I going to do?" I asked.

"You could coach," he said.

"I don't want to be no damn coach," I said. "I want to pitch and I know I can still do it just as good as anyone else on this team."

"Okay," Goose said as he laughed himself off to sleep.

I did not sleep that night. I stayed up the entire night, listening to Goose snore and thinking about what he had said. I was not ready to give up the rock and I damn sure did not want to coach.

The next morning I went to the ballpark before

anyone got there. I decided to test my arm by throwing the ball from the mound to the back stop. It still hurt like hell and I was scared.

Coach did not ask me to pitch the first game I was back, but he did ask me how I felt.

"Just fine," I said.

"Well, I'm giving you the rock tomorrow," he said. "They got some good hitters on that team. So make sure that you sleep well tonight and think through your pitching routine. They don't know you have been away. Just throw like your life depended on it."

"You can count on that," I said. Keep the faith, coach. I'm radio tuned in to a victory for our team."

The next day we played a doubleheader. I was scheduled to pitch the second game. We won the first easily and my stomach began to churn around the sixth inning of the game which we won easily six to four.

When I took the mound my heard was aching, my stomaching was upset and my arm felt like shit. There were about 20,000 people in the stands and they were watching me closely, as were my teammates and my coaches.

I had been with the Clowns for seven years and this was no way to lay down the gauntlet. When the first batter came to the plate I was rubbing the ball into my globe. Goose was talking as always and the other infielders urged me on.

The first pitch that my catcher called was a fastball. I called him off and requested that I know a slider. He signaled okay. I went into my windup and kicked my leg up in the air as I always did. The ball left my hand and I knew that I did not have anything. I did not last the inning.

I did not pitch again for four days. I was asked to do some relief work. I could get the pitch over the plate but my arm hurt like hell. My coach would not put me in until he knew that we had won the ball game.

I knew it was over. My career as a pitcher was over. I did not start another game that season. I just went in towards the end of a game and painfully throw as many pitches as I could, hoping that no one would hit the ball out of the park.

I thought about how my career in Negro League baseball had begun. A guy in the army had seen me pitch and asked me if I wanted to play professional baseball. I went to Detroit and stayed there for two days while the owners struggled to find the money to field a team. Later I joined the Cincinatti Crescents and they sold me to the Clowns.

I thought about the Pullman car porters who rode the trains with us and gave us the news of the day. They were mostly intellectuals who could not become college professors. For some reason, I also thought about Bebob, a midget who was a member of our team.'

But with all of the good memories, I knew after six years of big league baseball my time as a professional was over. Two nights after the last game that I pitch the coach asked me if I wanted a train ticket or bus ticket to go home. I told him that I wanted to take the train. The next day he gave me a ticket and an envelope with a half year's salary and said goodbye.

I knew I would miss the league greatly. Especially gentlemen of the game such as "Buck" O'Neil. He played fifteen years for the Kansas City Monarchs, one of the league's best teams. He seldom hit less than 350 and played a stellar first base. He managed in the league for the number of years and was so well thought of around baseball that he later became the first black coach for the Chicago Cubs. I called Buck and told him that I was leaving the game. He said a prayer for me and told me to take care of my family.

It was 1950 and I was finished. I had once dreamed of being in the Negro League Hall of Fame. But now I could only think of returning to Dallas and being with my family and friends.

One of my coaches came to visit me in Dallas. He was going to Japan to tour with the Harlem Globetrotters. He wanted me to help him with the team. He stayed in Dallas for two weeks, trying to convince me to make the trip. But I was dead set against it. I did not like basketball, had never been to Japan and I dislike flying.

I was not one to sit around the house. I liked being home with the family but I missed the road. I listened to ball games on radio, refereed local high school games and read the sports pages, trying to stay as close as I could to the life of a professional athlete.

The Dallas daily papers, like most papers in the country, carried very little about Negro baseball. Even though there were great players in our city like Ernie Banks, who went on the star with the Chicago Cubs, they received little notice.

Ernie was an exceptional ball player but he was not fond of the game and did not think of a life in professional baseball until the many talks we had about my experiences and the experiences of people like Goose Tatum, Josh Gibson and Satchel Paige. I believe that my influence led him to believe that she could be a professional baseball player.

While traveling on the road I often thought of how

great it would be if there was a newspaper devoted to Black Baseball. I knew quite a bit about baseball but nothing about journalism or the newspaper business. I did know if I asked people I could learn all that I needed to know about the business.

The first person I approached was Walter Travis, who worked in the grounds department at Booker T. Washington High School. Walter had an interest in starting a newspaper so we shared our ideas. He suggested that I talk to Jewel Ross McKenzie, the head of the journalism department at Booker T. It was one of the best pieces of advice that I ever received.

Ms. McKenzie suggested that I approach the owner of Riley's commercial printing on Ervay Street in downtown Dallas. I met with the owner, told him what I wanted to do and he told me to bring all of my information down to his place of business and he would show me how to get started.

That is how the Southwest Sporting Newspaper was born. It contained scores of games and profiles on athletes. It covered high school, college and professionals sports. I had connections with coaches and players and I had all of the information that I needed to keep the paper going.

Riley taught me the type of paper I should print on, the type of ink I should use and suggested deadlines for my paper, something that I knew very little about. The very first paper was published in the fall of 1951. It was eight pages and it sold for fifteen cents.

Once Riley printed it, I picked it up from his shop and packed it into my car. I delivered it to distribution points all over Dallas, including barbershops, schools and churches. Advertising paid for the printing of the paper, which I assembled alone and I even managed to have a few out of town subscribers who paid the price of subscription.

Bill Blair's friends include businesspeople, members
of the clergy, elected officials and many more

Bill Blair is one the most dapper men in Dallas

Bill Blair is admired by many in the Dallas community

People from throughout Texas attended the Martin Luther King Day Jr. Parade that Bill Blair founded

Members of the clergy have been honored
annually by Bill Blair and his newspaper

The Dallas District Attorney, Craig Watkins (r) was
counseled by Bill Blair before he sought office

Bill Blair has traditionally surrounded himself with
some of the city of Dallas' finest leaders

From his youth Bill Blair spent his Sundays in
church. He continues that practice today.

A former member of the U.S. Army, Bill Blair has
always honored members of the military

William Blair and his wife, left at the
wedding of one of their daughters

Mr and Mrs William Blair

Sometimes Bill Blair enjoyed relaxing

Blair signing over his papers to the University of Texas at Arlington

I was told to publish the paper on Fridays so that I could get grocery store advertising. The first two food chains to do business with me were Safeway and A&P Good Market. I sold each of them a full page of advertising for $100.00 per page.

Over the years the paper continued to grow. Athletes would send me pictures of themselves and profiles that they had written. The sports departments at area colleges also sent stories. At the beginning of each season I printed game schedules and reported news that readers could not get from reading the daily segregated newspapers.

Mine was the first all sports newspaper in Dallas. There was a black newspaper devoted to news and another devoted to gossip about preachers. We competed for readership and advertising with one another and the publisher got along very well.

I did not have an office in the very beginning. I assembled the stories and laid the paper out on the kitchen table in our home. Pieces of paper were all over the place. My children helped me and learned the newspaper business right there in our home. It was a wonderful learning experience for all of us.

Nine years after launching the Southwest Sporting News and associate, Lewis Fields said that I should change the name of the newspaper and expand its coverage to include more than sports. He said that people liked me and that they would respond favorably to a general interest newspaper that I produced.

I talked it over with my wife and a couple of close friends and decided that I would become I would broaden the coverage of my paper. I decided to change the name to Elite News. I liked the word Elite, since it implied being the best. The advertisers that supported me with the sports newspaper continue to support me.

There was one thing missing, however, I did not have any power brokers on my side and I knew that I would have to have them in my corner. I looked around the community and decided that I would approach the leadership of the faith community. They were among the most powerful people in the community. I

Men like Maynard Jackson Sr. and Caesar Clarke had helped to shape the spiritual life of Dallas. When they spoke the entire community took notice of what they said, blacks and whites. Reverend Jackson's son, Maynard, later became the mayor of Atlanta. The Senior Jackson started founded the Interdenominational Ministerial Alliances, a powerful organization of Black clergy.

I envisioned a relationship with the church community that was based on reliance and faith. I approached Reverend Wright, the president of the Alliance and told him of the vision that I had about the relationship between my paper and the faith community. I told him that I wanted to become the organization's "faithful partner."

He told me that he welcomed such a relationship and began to introduce me to some of the most powerful clergy leaders in the city of Dallas. Reverend Wright, raised in Dallas, was the pastor of the People's Baptist Church and a leader in the National Baptist Convention.

As President of the Alliance he worked directly with some of the most powerful business leaders, elected officials and lawyers in Dallas. When the powerful in north Dallas wanted something done in south Dallas they had to go throw Reverend Wright.

Reverend Wright understood politics and many of the first Black politicians elected to city-wide office in Dallas sought his blessing and that of the organization that he led. Reverend Wright took me by the hand and gave me a spiritual and political education.

Through Reverend Wright I met President Lyndon Baines Johnson, who sought Reverend Wright's counsel regularly. I also met Governor John Connnally and Senator Lloyd Bentsen because of him.

Among the powerful pastors that he introduced me to were Reverend M.L. Curry the pastor of the New St. Paul Baptist Church; Reverend C.B.T. Smith, the pastor of Golden Gate Baptist Church; Reverend E.C. Estell of St. John Missionary Baptist Church; Reverend E.K. Bailey of Concord Baptist Church; Bishop J.Neaul Haynes, the Presiding Bishop of the Texas Church of God In Christ; Apostle Lobias Murray and Dr. C.A.W. Clark who headed the Texas Baptist Convention.

Because of my relationship with Reverend Wright these men grew to trust me. They opened the doors of their churches to me. On any given Sunday I participated in three or four church services. I was given the title of "Brother Blair" by Reverend Wright. "You can trust this man," he told others.

At Reverend Wright's suggestion the motto of the Elite News became "the voice of the church community." The paper began to feature stories on pastors and members of their congregations. It became an outlet for church news and opinions of pastors. While some of the other papers in Dallas were critical of churches, I lifted them up.

REVEREND WRIGHT TOOK ME WHEREVER HE traveled in the state of Texas and beyond. I became his driver and his confidant. I listened closely in the car as he counseled younger ministers who sometimes traveled with us advising them on how to handle problems in their churches or families. His advice was always the same. "Take this to your altar," he told them. "Trust in the Lord he will make a way for you."

Reverend Wright headed a bi-racial twelve person committee that met regularly to discuss problems that were facing minorities in Dallas. The committee also met with members of the white power structure and negotiated agreements around issues of fair housing and accommodations. The Chief of Police always attended the meetings and Reverend Wright always pointed out how it was important that the police and the community respect one another.

When other cities experienced civil disturbances Dallas remained quiet. That was largely due to power brokers such as Reverend Wright who told city leaders about the demands of the minority communities before things spilled out into the streets. Reverend Wright had relationships with everyone. One of his closest allies was Lew Sterett, a county judge who many thought was a closeted member of the Klan.

Reverend Wright and Sterett worked together to get Blacks hired in the Dallas County Courthouse and in the tax assessor's office. His lieutenants at mass meetings were Reverend Estell, Dr. B. R. Riley and a lawyer named W.J. Durham. The three of them were successful in getting the state fair and public transportation integrated.

There were few changes that took place in the public life of Dallas without the involvement of Reverend Wright and powerful members of the clergy that he led. My paper benefited tremendously from the relationship that I had with Reverend Wright. He never told me what to Wright in my paper, but he always pointed me in the correct direction.

Reverend Wright was not liked by everyone. There were those who accused him of being an Uncle Tom and a racial crumb snatcher but he persevered and kept his head up. Extremely loyal, he once threatened to quit an organization of ministers if they turned their backs on a printer who did business with them when they could not afford to pay their bills.

When the preachers went against Reverend Wright's counsel he formed another ministerial organization to compete with them. He did not do it out of spite. He did it because he did not know if he could trust any of them any longer.

Reverend Wright was instrumental in the building of a number of high schools for Black and the Martin Luther King Community Center near Fair Park. Members of his congregation knew that they could call him day or night and he would be there. Whether it was someone who was rushed to the hospital or someone who had experienced a sudden death in their family, they knew that Reverend Wright would soon be at their side with a prayer that would sustain them during a difficult time, or with a shoulder that they could lean on when they could not stand by themselves.

It seemed that fighting for change came natural for Reverend Wright. He was unafraid. He often told me about his late father, Reverend C.M. Wright who confronted the city's loan sharks who were taking advantage of poor people.

The senior Wright was successful in his fight against the loan sharks, but his family suffered. He was unable to get any personal credit an experienced economic harm. "Blair, my father did not mind suffering if it meant that the community improved," Reverend Wright would say.

A graduate of Lincoln High School, Reverend Wright was engaged in a battle that saved his Alma Mata. His pulpit at the Peoples Baptist Church was a home for presidents like Jimmy Carter, U.S. Senators like Lloyd Bentsen and Texas Governors such as Dolph Briscoe.

Reverend Wright taught me many things about business and about life. One thing that he taught me was the importance of having a good lawyer. The legal mind that Reverend Wright preferred who stood at his side was W.J. Durham, a native of Sulphur Springs, Texas who attended Emporia State College in Kansas.

After being admitted to the Texas Bar in 1926, Durham established a law practice in Sherman, Texas. His presence attracted the attention of groups such as the Klan as he fought to end desegregation laws. His office was burned down but he was not deterred.

In the1940s he worked to end housing discrimnatin in South Dallas, He also was one of the lead attorneys in a case that integrated the University of Texas Law School. When Reverend Wright needed a committed legal mind, he turned to Durham. Taking the lead from Reverend Wright, whenever I needed a legal mind in business, I turned to Mr. Durham. It was a decision that I did not live to regret.

I admired Durham. He was clever and always eager to assist people such as Reverend Wright who was viewed as a champion in the community. I often sat in meetings and listened as they discussed political, social and legal issues. In the beginning I understood little of what they were talking about. I had only completed the

12th grade and had spent my formative years on the road as a professional athlete.

But Reverend Wright always told me to listen intently and to keep a notebook where I wrote down words and phrases that were new to me. After most of the meetings I rushed, found a dictionary and imagined that I had taken part in the conversations.

I always told my wife that I had been in discussions with Reverend Wright and other civic leaders. I did not tell her that I was like a first grader listening as the

Intellectual giants in the room spoke and planned strategy. I sometimes felt as though I had cheated myself by not going to college, but there was little I could do. I had a wife and children who were depending of me for their livelihood.

Another of the men who Reverend Wright often met with and counseled was Antonio Maceo Smith, a business owner, teacher and newspaper executive who lived in Dallas.

Professor Smith, as some of us called him, mobilized Black people to make improvements in education, employment and business development. He chaired the southwest area YMCA council, served on the board of directors of the Dallas Urban League, was a trustee of Bishop College and served on the board of directors of the National Conference of Christians and Jews.

He worked tirelessly to force the city to hire Black police officers. When he talked he looked an observer straight in the eye, his heavy black glasses early falling from his nose. He was comfortable working from center stage and from behind the curtains. He and men like Reverend Wright their egos in their back pockets when they were in meetings.

As I grew closer to the faith community a few of the competing publishers grew angry with me. One accused me of being a front for the frailties of the faith community. Another suggested that I was on Reverend Wright's payroll.

One publisher in particular continued to publish lies about certain members of the clergy, impugning their characters and suggesting that they preached one thing but lived differently in their personal lives. There are four of us who had papers and I got a long with most of them. But there was one publisher whose personal life was in the gutter.

He believed in getting on the public and the business community anyway that he could. He was once accused of forging the signature of a civil rights leader on a letter to Dallas area business owners, threatening them with a boycott of their

Businesses if they did not advertiser with him. On another occasion he took $50,000 from a Texas elected official do some political work. The official later discovered the materials that the publisher was supposed to distribute were kept in a closet in his office. He was charged with theft and sentenced to a jail term.

I founded out about his charged and published news of it in my newspaper. When he asked me to stop I told him that I was simply exercising my right as a publisher in a democracy. If it had been anyone else I would have stopped printing the stories but my hatred for him was so intense that I did not care what happened to him or his family.

He died while serving probation for his crime. I was asked to speak on behalf of the city's publishers at his funeral but my hatred for him was so intense that I refused the request and did not attend the service. Quite frankly I was glad that he was gone. He had been a thorn in my side for many years and we had become bitter foes.

While working with Reverend Wright and other ministers I heard many sermons about forgiveness but I was not able to bring myself to forgive this man, the things that he had done to me and others and the lies that he told. I knew that it was wrong to hate him but I could not help myself. I simply did not like him.

Over the years my family had continue to grow. My eldest son, Sandy, was a student and instructor at Howard University in Washington, D.C. The others all completed high school and chose various professions.

None of my children seemed particularly interested in following me into the newspaper business. I was okay with that. There were times when I was not sure that I had made the best decision for my own life. I was happy that they were happy.

Mozelle had entered the catering business, providing food and services for individuals and companies throughout North Texas. The kids seemed eager to join her in the food services business. At parties they could dress up in formal wear and eat all of the food that they wanted.

They also had the opportunity visit some of the finest homes in Dallas and work in the some of the most luxurious hotels. I could offer them a hamburger at McDonalds but nowhere near the ambience that my wife afforded them.

On a night when Mozelle had a party, five or six of the children would pile into a car and ride with her t the venue. They all pitched in and conducted themselves as real owners. I think that one day they saw themselves as owning a food empire.

While working the parties they met many types of people, particularly in the white community. They were exposed to wealthy Jewish people in North Texas, some of whom were best friends with their mother. They visited some of the homes more than once and became friends with the children of their mother's customers.

From time to time Mozelle would come home with bags of used clothing, some of its from the finest stores in Dallas. But I did not like the idea of my children or my wife wearing something that another person had worn or had out grown. I objected to the practice but my wife ignored me and my children were thrilled with the clothing for the most part.

One time my wife brought home a pair of size eight Stacey Adams high top boots. They were black and only slightly used. When she and the children went to sleep that night I tried them on and they were a perfect fit. But my conscience would not allow me to keep them. The next morning I reluctantly gave them to Mozelle and told her to tell her friends not to send me shoes anymore.

I had always been very proud and I really needed a pair of shoes. The two pairs that I had both had worn soles and I could have really used them. I did not have enough money to purchase a decent apri of shoes. Most of my money went into my family and to running the Elite News.

Sandy was always a very bright young man. When he was growing I thought he had a future in political life. Perhaps he could be the first African American mayor of Dallas, I thought, or perhaps a college president. The sky was the limit for him. He married a wonderful young woman and had two lovely children.

One of the reasons I took the accident so hard that took his life and those of his family were that my expectation for him were so high and he was my first born. I taught him how to play baseball although I did not want him to have the type of life that I experienced in the Negro Baseball League.

He and his family were leaving our home when their small car was attacked by a sudden storm. The water carried the car and none of them could get out. All of them were killed, but his wife's body was not found for sixth months from the day of the accident.

I was in a daze and do did not want to attend the funeral where my son and his children were being eulogized. I was briefly angry at God because Sandy was such a nice person and I knew terrible people who were still walking the streets.

Once, while alone, I asked God why He had taken Sandy and nearly cursed him. I quickly remembered something that my spiritual mentor, Reverence Wright, had once told a young minister who had just lost his home and his church.

"God will make a way for you doing the darkest hour and during the longest night." His words became a solid foundation for me. They helped to carry me during a time when I began to question whether or not God was, in fact, on the side of those who believe in justice, goodness and charity. Sandy was the type of individual who would give you his last dime if you should him a need. He was an educated man. While watching him grow up I thought he would become the first African American Mayor of Dallas. He was a person who captivated all of those he met.

The day of the funeral was one of the most difficult of my life. We had not found his wife's body so we decided to go ahead with the service. My friends at the Golden Gate Funeral Home handled the service with great dignity.

The church was packed. Many of my pastor friends came out to console me and my family. They said wonderful things about "my special little boy" and his family. His body was in a bronze coffin and those of his children were in smaller coffins surrounding him

I kept my eyes close during most of the service and thought of the times when I taught him how to catch a ball, how to throw a runner out, how to ride a bicycle and how to dance. He loved to dance. His mother cried her heart out during the service. She and Sandy were very close and she loved her grandchildren.

When we buried them, it seemed as if all of Dallas was at the cemetery. We had a repast and then I went home to think of Sandy and the impact that he dad on my life. Some months later we found the remains of his wife. We buried her next to her husband and her children.

In addition to the church I worked with Civil Rights organizations in Dallas. One of the groups that I supported quietly was the NAACP. Juanita Jewell Craft, more than anyone else in the city, helped to mold the group.

In 1945, just after the War, Mrs. Craft directed a membership drive that increased NAACP membership to more than 8,000. She became a leader of the group in Texas and helped to organize chapter throughout the state.

Two years after the membership drive she became the youth director for the NAACP throughout Texas. She encouraged young people to study and began campaigns to integrate the University of Texas at Austin and North

Texas State University in Denton. Largely because of her efforts, the national organization brought its international convention to Dallas in 1954.

She also began a campaign to integrate the Texas State Fair. For as long as I could remember, Blacks only had one day at the fair. She was a compelling speaker and was elected to the Dallas City Council.

She worked hand in hand with others like Dr. H.I Holland, an educator who came to Dallas to teacher at Booker T. Washington High School in 1926. He was the principal of a number of elementary schools and later became the principal at Lincoln High School from 1955 until 1963.

Dr. Holland encouraged young people to seek greatness. He served as a board member of the Moorland YMCA and was a supporter of Big Brothers of America. Numerous young people in Dallas decided to pursue higher education because of Dr. Moreland.

Another Dallas leader who worked with Mrs. Craft was A. Maceo Smith. One of fourteen children raised in Texarkana, Dr. Smith was graduated from Fisk University and New York University.

He was a man of great intellect who also published a newspaper and owned an advertising agency. He worked for the federal government for nearly two decades and used his impressive interpersonal skills to help reshape Dallas during the 1940s, 1950s and 1950s. A member of the trustee board at Bishop College, he was the first Black person to become chairman of the Southwest Area YMCA Council. He was also the president of the Dallas Urban League and was the national president of the Alpha Phi Alpha fraternity.

I featured people like Dr. Holland, Dr. Smith and Mrs.

Craft in my newspaper. I used it as a tool that allowed them to get their messages to the larger community. Where they could, they helped me to secure advertising. I could call any of them day or night. They were invaluable to the success that my newspaper experienced.

Because my newspaper was positive it was welcomed among the clergy and the politically powerful. There had been a newspaper named The Brother's Eye. It was a scandal sheet that reported the alleged activities of pastors outside of their churches.

It was published by a very prominent citizen whose father-in-law was Booker T Washington, the great educator. The publisher cared very little about the community. His sole objective was to sell newspapers. A typical story began "Reverend Able, whose wife is away from Dallas for a conference, was seen coming out of Sister Sampson's house at three in the morning. The pastor appeared to be in a hurry, his Bible in one hand and shoes in the other. We wonder what the people of his church would think if they saw a picture of him running in the Sunday bulletin.

The preachers loathed the man and some of them did all they could to have him arrested. A couple plotted to have him shot but nothing came of it. I remember Dr. Wright telling me that my paper should be a "counter balance to that filth."

And that is what I tried to do. On some Sunday I would visit five churches. I phone the paper the night before if he had a telephone and told him that I was coming.

The minutes I hit a sanctuary the services stopped and I was announced. The Elite News had become the official voice of the faith community and I did not know at the time the power of the voice that my publication had become.

Churches started to advertise their events in the mayor. Pastor wanted their pictures place in the paper with their order of services. I was more than happy to oblige them.

IT WAS NOT LONG BEFORE NEARLY one quarter of the paper was devoted to religious advertising and church listings. Some of my competitors complained that I had "sold out" to the preaching community, but I ignored them. It was a simple business decision, made with of the most powerful ministers ever to have lived I Dallas, Reverend S. M.Wright.

I will never forget the day that Reverend Wright called me and told me that there was some business downtown that he needed me to take care of for him. I quickly got into the car and drove to his office.

Reverend Wright was concluding a counseling session with one of his members who had difficulty in this third marriage. I had met the man before. I believe he worked with the city, but was not sure.

I overhead Reverend Wright telling him that had to do all that he could to make his marriage work. The man thanked him and then quickly walked passed me in the hallway.

"Blair, ministry is a difficult thing sometimes," Reverend Wright said. "It is more than just preaching on Sunday morning. It is giving your lives to the people who are members of your flock."

Reverend Wright looked tired. His days were often fifteen hours long. He had little time for his family and he did not eat properly, fried foods, baked cakes and pies and sweet tea. But he seldom gave any thought to himself. He was always concerned about the "other guy" who was in need of assistance.

"Blair," he said. "I need you to go downtown and speak with a prosecutor in the district attorney's office. There is a friend of mine who made a mistake and he needs some help. I cannot afford to go down there myself but the man downtown knows who you are and he knows that you will be coming down to take care of something for me."

"What exactly do I ask him?" I asked.

"Just tell him that my friend made a mistake and that he and his family need a break," Reverend Wright said.

"What is the name of the friend?"

"He will know," Reverend Wright said.

"Just tell him that I said to go easy on the man for me."

"Is that all that I need to tell him?"

"That's all I want you to do," he said.

"I'll take care of it," I said.

"You will need to get down there before court starts," he said. "His office is on the third floor."

"I've got my marching orders," I said.

"Well then get marching."

The next morning I called a taxi and rode downtown because I did not want to worry about parking. I told the driver to wait for me and that I would take care of him.

"How long are you going to be, Mr. Blair?" he asked.

"I won't be long. Just wait for me out here and I will make it worth your while," I said.

"Okay, Mr. Blair. I will be here."

I walked inside the building and took the steps up to the third floor. The assistant was waiting for me.

"Come into my office," he said

"Thank you," I said.

"You know," he said. "This meeting never happened."

"Yes, I know," I said. "It's off the record."

"No it never happened," he said.

"I understand."

I gave the prosecutor the name of the man that Reverend Wright wanted to help. He looked at it once and said that he would handle it.

"Tell Reverend Wright that everything is under control and to tell his friend that he can stop sweating," he said.

"I most certainly will," I said.

"Come back and see me again if the Reverend sends you," he said. "What type of business are you in?"

"I am a newspaper publisher," I said.

"What is the name of the paper?"

"Elite," I said.

"I think I heard of it," he said. "You take care."

"I will," I said and rushed out of the door.

The taxi driver was waiting for me on the side of the building where he left me. He had his blinkers and was reading a Jet Magazine.

"How did things go Mr. Blair?" he asked me.

"Oh, just fine," I said. "I don't think I will be having any more problems out of the county."

"It must be good to have friends downtown," he said as he laid the Jet on the seat beside me.

"Yes, the contacts can come in handy," I said.

"Where do you want to go?"

"Back to my office," I said.

THE NEWSPAPER WAS A GOOD BASE in the community. For years I tried to get my children to take an interest in the paper but their time was consumed with other activities.

My sons went to college and wanted to become business owners. Debra got married and began to raise a family. My youngest son seemed destined for politics but seemed more interested in creating a name for himself rather than following his old man's line of work.

My newspaper grew as Dallas continued to grow. The Dallas Black Chamber of Commerce was the largest and most powerful Black Chamber in the country. Organized in 1926, its members elected Helen Giddings, who later became a state representative, as its first President. That was a milestone for a southern city.

Some of its early members, E.J. Crawford, Dr. L.G. Pinkston, Dr. W.K. Flowers, Dr. R.T. Hamilton and R.A. Hester were people of vision and pillars of the community. I did not have the social standing of some of these commercial titans but I was proud of what they had been able to do.

There were nights when I sat in my office near Fair Park and wondered how I was going to pay to have my paper printed and I thought of the work of the Black Chamber and I was encouraged.

I would also think of women such as Mrs. Pearl C. Anderson, whose grandparents were slaves. Much of the valuable property in downtown Dallas was given to the city by Mrs. Anderson who with her late husband, John Wesley, had amassed a fortune. She was one of the largest donors to charities in the city.

I knew that the paper had to have events associated with it that would highlight the contributions of people in the community. I started the Elite News Awards in 1975 that cited the contributions that various people made to the life of Dallas.

YEARS LATER, RECOGNIZING THAT NO ONE had recognized the significant contributions that the church had made the Dallas, I organized the Elite News Religious Hall of

Fame. Its first inductees included some of finest preachers in Dallas.

There were some who resented the fact that I started events. Most of them started out very small. Some of them did not work but I knew that I could make them work with hard work and the assistant of the pastors who had become my friends over the years.

I had always had a respect for Dr. Martin Luther King Jr. I first learned of him while listening to preachers such as Caesar Clarke speak about him. Not all ministers considered Dr. King a friend. Many of them were jealous and others held him in contempt.

I first heard him speak at the Good Street Church and was impressed with his eloquence and his message. I knew that he was for real. Dr. King sacrificed his family and his life for the civil rights movement and for others. He could have made a fortune as a preacher but he was not into ministry for money. He was in it for service.

A little bit of me died when he was killed in Memphis while helping garbage workers. The genius of Dr. King was that he was for the little person. When I thought of him I thought of why I had started the Elite Newspaper.

I had always enjoyed parades and one night I thought that I should start a parade named for Dr. King. I spoke to a number of people about it and received little encouragement, but I decided that I would go ahead with our without them.

In 1986 on Dr. King's birthday I held the first Dr. Martin Luther King Jr. parade and festival. The parade route started on Martin Luther king. We had five cars one marching band and one drummer.

I marched at the head of the parade with several of my clergy friends. People stopped and looked at us as if we were fools. I marched as though there were five thousands marchers behind me. I knew that one day it would be a stable of life in Dallas.

Ideas like the Hall of Fame, which was started in 1999, and the King Parade came easily to me. The most difficult part was getting others to buy into your idea. Most of the time they were against your idea, largely because it was not their own. I had learned while playing baseball that the crowd would sometimes be against me but that did not keep me from performing the best I could.

I carried pictures of the parade and the Hall of Fame events in the paper, hoping that they would grow. Before long I began to receive calls from preachers who wanted to be included in the Hall of Fame and from marching bands that wanted to participate in the parade. Their calls warmed my heart and allowed both events to grow.

The response taught me a lesson that I had learned a long time ago as a baseball player. Life was very much like a baseball game. It was nine innings long. It did not matter if you were down by five runs in the bottom of the third inning. You still had several times to bat. And just because you were behind did not give you the right to give up. The struggle continued no matter what the score.

For the most part my newspaper depended on advertisers in the Black Community and some small white owned businesses. It was rare that a major downtown business, although many Blacks supported them, came to advertise with papers like the Elite News.

When I did make contact with them they always made excuses or they simply took an ad once or twice during the year. I was accustomed to disappointment. I remembered, well, the days of only being able to go to the fair on a single day. So, I did not mind rejection.

ONE OF THE BEST DAYS OCCURRED in 1999 when my third oldest son, Randy, came to me and said that he wanted to work with the newspaper. Prior to then he had worked for a fast food company as a manager.

When he realized that his abilities far surpassed his career opportunities he decided that he would come into the newspaper business with me. I was thrilled when he sat down to talk.

Randy had some brilliant ideas about the paper. He suggested that we increase our circulation, change the look of the paper and run more political stories. I liked his ideas and his enthusiasm. It was very clear to me that he was willing to pour his entire soul into the paper. And he did.

There were days when I arrived at the paper only to find Randy already at his desk. He had some new ideas for our designer, Roman Ross, and he even suggested that I start a regular column in the newspaper. He suggested that we start a golf tournament and increase our advertising rates.

Initially, I thought that we were not ready for many of Randy's ideas but I managed to listen to him and many of them proved to be sound and increased the cash flow of the paper.

Randy took over things like the management of the Martin Luther king Jr. Parade and represented the Elite News at various civic and business meetings. He contacted advertising in Dallas City Hall and in Dallas County. Before long began to reap additional revenue from both of these governmental bodies.

A national born salesman, Randy was good at making friends and influencing people. He brought new talent into the Elite News circle, writers such as Rufus

Shaw and marketing talent such as Big Mark Jones. They breathed new breath into the Elite News and helped to change the image in the community.

Randy believed that I was too dependent on the church community and he and I argued in the beginning about his position. I yelled at him and he yelled at me, but we never lost sight of the fact that I was his father and he was my son.

We both understood that we had always been there for one another. When he was a student at Prairie View I did all that I could to make his college experience a pleasant one.

One he called me and told me the story of a classmate who was using drugs. He said that he was afraid that the young man was a few months away from death and wanted to know what he should do to keep him from killing himself.

I told him not to give up on his friend but be prepared to lose him if it came to that. When I said that a silence fell over the phone. Randy wanted to know if that meant that he should not care about his friend. I told him that he should care for him, but that he should not be a fool about it.

I believe the young man's name was Fred who had been raised in a large east coast city. Randy said that he had started using drugs after experimenting with them at a fraternity party.

Randy had attended the same party but told me that he refused the drugs that the older students offered him and other first year students. I just knew that it was not right and that you would be disappointed with me," he said. I j knew that I would be letting you down if I tried the drugs.

I told Randy that I was proud of him and that trying drugs would have been a mistake. I am proud of you, I said. We both were silent for a moment, something that was rare for the two of us. He said that he would keep trying with his friend, Fred.

FRED CONTINUED TO DO DRUGS AND even stole some things from other students on the college campus, but Randy did not give up on him and continue to encourage him. He brought him to the business on a couple of occasions when they had breaks from school and asked me about giving him a job. He wanted to stay in the south and did not want to return home to the north.

I told him if I heard good things about his work I would consider teaching him the publishing business. You and Randy can work together, I told him. He liked the idea and was always very respectful.

Randy worked with his friend as though he was his own child. He made sure that he had money and that he stayed always from alcohol and liquor. My son became his friend's big brother, and I was very proud of the way that he looked after his friend. Actually, Randy saved the young man from killing himself.

Fred stopped taking drugs. Actually I think that Randy told him that either he could allow drugs to kill him or Randy would do it himself. While he was not serious, Fred took it as a serious threat. He stopped when he realized that Randy was not going to have any more of the foolishness.

Fred received his degree and did return north. He settled in a business and did real well for himself. I do not think that he would have survived had it not been for Randy's intervention in his life.

Our relationship was far from smooth. It was at sometimes rocky. There we were two businessmen---one from the old school and the other from the new school who saw things differently. We both wanted to see the newspaper success but we had different visions as to how it should be done.

Randy was not stingy with the money that he made while working with the Elite News. When the newspaper fell on difficult times he went into his pocket and into his family's to pay the bills. I appreciate it greatly, but my pride never allowed me to tell him that.

NOT LISTENING TO MY SON AND the suggestions that he had for the newspaper was a huge mistake. I often treated him like a business partner that I did not trust rather than a son who was serious about making a difference in the family business and taking it over in the future.

I had been brought up in a very hard fashion and I treated my son sometimes as he was my enemy and not someone who was close to me who simply disagreed with the way that I wanted to do things. I think that he understood me more than I understood him. And there were times when he treated me far better than I treated him.

Randy brought much need into the papers such as Mark Jones and Corey Toney. Initially, I was suspicious of them and their intentions. But as I grew closer to them I realized that they were seriously interested in the success of the newspaper and my personal success.

Randy introduced concepts such as Elite News community forums and education programs for young people, something in which he had a particular interest. In fact, he took an iner5st in the educations of all of his nieces and nephews. It was something that he liked to do. He attended all of their graduations, birthday parties and special events. He was present at times when I was noticeably absent.

With Randy's ideas special programs such as the Hall of Fame and the King Parade grew significantly. In fact, one year we had 250,000 people along the parade route with a parade that last four hours. It was a long way from four cars and one man beating a drum

THE THING I LIKED MOST ABOUT Randy was that he had vision. Going to college at Prairie View had been very good for him. I encouraged him to run for politics and to attempt to head political organizations. The first attempts at seeking office were unsuccessful, but he landed a seat on the Dallas County Board of Education and helped to change the educational philosophy of the school district.

When the paper ran into legal difficulties it was Randy, once again, who went into his family's savings and made certain that we paid our obligations. He encouraged his own children to pursue education and all of them were success. One of them, a grandson who I became very proud of, became the president of the student body at Prairie View College.

I sensed that Randy's involvement in the paper caused him difficulty at home, but he was committed to him although I was at times his chief nemesis. I never told him before he died, but he was the single most important thing that happened to the Elite News. His involvement was greater than our relationship with Reverend Wright and the powerful ministers that we aligned ourselves with.

When I first told Randy about the idea of the Religious Hall of Fame, he was not one hundred percent sold on it but he told me that he would help me with the ideas and he did everything that he could to make it successful year after year.

He helped me to decide which ministers should be honored and always hosted the enhanced the quality of the programs. He involved his children in helping him with the paper just as I did with a few of my children when I first when into the publishing business. It was frequently my dream that he learned that from me.

I had preached involving family in business and believed that it was the right thing to do. I think that Randy listened and tried to involve his brothers and sister, but things do not always work out amongst siblings and they did not work well among the Blair children. I watched them fight but was unable to take a side.

For years some of my children stayed away from the business. Much of it was my fault. I had not drawn up a family will and had not made clear just who it was that I wanted to have run the business should something happened to me. I l alwso was nto a good manager of the competition that surfaced among them.

I felt if the children worked together we could produce a superior product to any other being produced in Dallas, including the daily newspaper, but I could not get them to come together.

They did, from time to time, pitch in on the various projects such as a golf tournament, the Hall of Fame and the educational programs but I could tell that their hearts were not in it the projects and while they participated, it was not full participation. It was partial and sometimes half hearted.

Randy expanded the reach of the newspaper. For the first time, we began to regularly appear in north Dallas and even in Ft. Worth. We began to receive adverting inquiries from parts of town where had never had a presence. Major supermarkets and clothing stores began to advertise. It was largely due to Randy's influence.

Mozelle and I had a long standing policy. I would not get involved in her catering business if she did not get involved in my newspaper. That was the way it was from the time that I started Southwest Sporting News when I returned from playing Major League Baseball.

Mozelle had a keen mind for detail. While working in the Negro Baseball leagues she excelled as keeping a balance sheet and setting schedules. In our home over the years she was closer to the children that I was as I frequently had meetings that conflicted with their events. She made certain she was always present at the sporting events, dances and church functions. On Sundays led the Blair delegation to St. Paul AME where she groomed Randy for leadership.

Mozelle grew her catering business from making a few cakes for certain customers to doing entire five course dinners. Over the years she became one of the most sought after caterers in business, color notwithstanding.

Mozelle's parents had been business owners who understood the importance of having something that they could call their own. That sense of entrepreneurship was passed to my wife.

Her business was very well known in the wealthier sections of town, for its service and the quality of its foods. Once, a wealthy couple offered Mozelle the opportunity to take the entire family to the Caribbean and open up a restaurant. When she came to me with the idea, I would have none of it.

Unlike me she was very good at developing

relationships. Once, when there was talk of riots breaking out in South Dallas she was involved by a white couple to bring the entire family to their home until things cooled off in our section of the town. After talking with me, she told the couple that we were content to remain where we were.

Her people skills were much better than mine. In high school she was elected beauty queen two years in a row. I was very lucky to have her as my wife. When I first proposed marriage I was afraid that she would turn me down, but she agreed to be my wife and helped me to raise a family and grow a business.

On evenings when she had more than one event, the children split into groups and worked the functions.

It was on such a night that we lost Sandy, his wife and children. Sandy had worked a function and was visitng with my daughter Debroah and her family in their home. It was early in the morning and Sandy decided to drive him with his family.

He had to get up early the next morning to work on a communications project. It had been raining for most of the day and when Sandy and his family reached the A small bridge where a whale of water confronted their car. They did not stand a chance. The water drove the car over the embankment and carried it for a few hundred yards before depositing Sandy and his lovely children on the shores of the river.

It was my daughter, Deborah, who called me to tell me of the tragedy. It was one of the worse moments of my life. I did not want to believe it when she told me that his body and those of his two children had been found. All I remember saying was "…..my Sandy, my Sandy."

I knew that I had to console Mozelle and the other children but my soul was in shock. I had decided that I could not cry in public. I recalled the first baseball that I threw to Sandy and the first time that I took him for a wagon ride.

As a boy, Sandy was a very special child. He was very smart and question. He wanted to know about the newspaper business and why I devoted so much of to business enterprise.

For years, precisely ten, it was the three of us, Sandy, Mozelle and me who shared our home. His coming into the world was a pleasant surpirse to me and my wife. His birth slowed my life down and exacted that I find even greater purpose for living. When he left me, I felt as though a part of my soul departed. It would be the same way when Randy died from cancer years later.

Now, I find myself in the twilight of my life. I am proud of many things that I have done and saddened by some. I take life one day at a time.

I was astonished when a local university, the University of Texas at Arlington, requested that my personal papers be catalogued by them. It meant that my life would live forever, something that I always wanted.

I felt distinguished on the morning that members of my family, members of the public, the media and administrators from the university gathered in the library of the university to witness my signing over my papers.

It meant that my contributions to life would last forever. A university spokesperson, Dr.Dulaney, said that it was one of the most significant collections that the university had acquired. When my turn came to speak I was speechless, something new to me.

News of my donation was broadcast across the state and country. I felt a sense of joy and satisfaction knowing that a Negro Baseball League pitcher whose best pitch was called twelve to six would live forever.

Made in the USA
Coppell, TX
17 November 2023

24369320R00059